Circle Time Resources

More games with word and picture cards
to vary Circle Time activities.

compiled by

George Robinson and Barbara Maines

ISBN 1 873 942 37 0

Lucky Duck Publishing Ltd
3 Thorndale Mews, Clifton, Bristol, BS8 2HX

Tel: 0117 973 2881
Fax: 0117 973 1707

Website: www.luckyduck.co.uk

Reprinted August 1999, April 2000, March 2001, October 2001, February 2003.

Printed in England by The Book Factory, Essex, SS13 1LJ

Contents

Foreword

At the end of the video 'Coming Round to Circle Time', Robinson and Maines (1995), a smiling teacher says, "I think Circle Time is wonderful!" We agree and we strive to enthuse others through our publications and inset training days. As we visit schools we are continually amazed and delighted by the ways in which facilitators re-invent and recreate Circle Time in many forms, remaining true to the essential principle of unconditional acceptance of the members of the circle.

Holding this principle dear it is therefore with great dismay that we observe, in some schools, the involvement of Circle Time into the school discipline policy where sanctions and rewards become part of the Circle Time procedures.

Ballard (1982) identifies ten value statements and suggests that if teachers do not share these they will have difficulty in conducting Circle Time. The fourth of these value statements is:

> "4. *circletime Is not therapy. it is not to be seen as a "treatment" of any kind .... we are not solving problems in a circletime session, but building skills of awareness. circletime is an educational model, and belongs in a school curriculum along with the other content areas. it requires no esoteric leader skills such as are required for counseling or doing therapy or treatment of any kind. no problem, in fact, is assumed. the teacher does not bring to the circle a "something-is-wrong-and-needs-fixing" problem mentality, and hence is not interested in analyzing, probing or psychologyzing kids. it is designed to be done by teachers with no special background other than a caring for children and an appreciation of the role of affective development in a child's experience. our recommendation, on the other hand, as previously stated, is that the user of this handbook have attended a workshop so as to be thoroughly grounded in the goals and methods. (our experience is that people who simply pick up a book and start leading circles sometimes do so with the mistaken intention of doing some sort of problem-solving with students for instance, doing circles to "reduce discipline problems".*

Ballard (1982)

note: the use of lower case letters throughout is a feature of the original text.

If you are already using Circle Time and have been taught to incorporate a behaviourist element such as earning and losing of Golden Time, Mosely (1996) then we would urge you to visit the original writing and inspirational concepts of Ballard and remember that all the British writers who publish material on Circle Time, including those with Lucky Duck, did not invent it. They have Ballard to

thank and would do well to acknowledge him and stand by his principals.
When Circle Time is well established it is interesting to see how the role of the facilitator, often a teacher who at other times of the day may be implementing a discipline policy, becomes less authoritarian. The participants accept responsibility and democracy as integral to the process. This does not mean that unacceptable behaviour is ignored, but that it is dealt with within the circle. It is also essential that unacceptable behaviours which happened at other times are not brought into circle time. The group might focus activities on a theme such as aggression in the playground but the specific behaviour of one or more children, discussed in a way which shames or stigmatises, is not the business of the circle group.

This publication provides a series of additional games and activities which might introduce new ideas or revive a flagging session. They are "add-ons", congruent with the aims of circle time. They are provided in book format on paper. The facilitator can choose to copy onto paper as a disposable resource or to reproduce on to card and laminate to make a more permanent item of equipment.

Circle Time and Emotional Literacy

The publication of Emotional IQ by Daniel Goleman (1995) validates the allocation of time and resources to the teaching of a curriculum which includes awareness of self, awareness of others and understanding and competence in managing group process and relationships.

> *"..much recent research has shown that all pupils need and will benefit from becoming emotionally literate and in developing adequate social and emotional skills, in order to be able to modify their own behaviour. (Greenberg and Kusche 1993, Elias and Calbby 1992). Schools have a clear focus and a required commitment to teaching the curriculum and basic skills, i.e. the three 'Rs'. It is becoming increasingly evident, however, that without a further commitment to teaching the fourth 'R' i.e. life and social skills of problem solving, empathy, co-operation and emotional literacy, schools will be failing many pupils. Without these skills and the sense of personal identity, self esteem and self control that can result from focusing upon them, some pupils will also not develop the academic and basic literacy skills they require in order to reach their full potential."*

Rae, T, (1998)

Circle Time is a process - it is content free. It provides the framework into which to place the emotional literacy curriculum.

How to use the cards

When your Circle Time is well established the young people will have practised and become competent in the skills needed for games and activities. These resources are intended as an addition or variation to use occasionally, to make a change, revive a "low" session.

In order to provide a reasonable priced resource the cards are printed onto paper with a licence to copy issued to the purchaser. This allows for
- photocopying on to paper for using once only
- copying onto card or sticking onto card and laminating to make a permanent set.

We have included some ideas for ways in which each set can be used but we are sure that many more games and activities will be devised. If you have any that you would like to send us then we will consider including them for the next edition and reference you as the source.

Activities using the Sentence Completion cards

Sentence completion is a standard and essential activity for Circle Time. One of its values lies in the repetition of the same sentence start;

Today I am feeling...

My Favourite TV programme is...

I am worried about....

so that children

- hear it frequently
- listen to a variety of endings
- reflect upon the answers of others
- become confident to give an answer.

Any variations on this activity are not intended to substitute the original but to add an alternative.

List of Sentences

A friend is.....
A quality I look for in a friend is......
Something I like to do with friends is......
Something I like to do with my best friend is......
The sort of people I like best are....
The sort of person I would trust is....
I respect friends who.....
If a friend has deceived me.....
The way I show my friends I'm angry is......
I laugh with my friends about......
Something my friends do that makes me laugh is.....
The kind of behaviour I would expect from my friends towards me is......
The kind of behaviour I prefer to see from my friends when we are out is.....
If my friends fall out I try to get them back together by....
An irritating habit that would turn me off could be....
Friends take advantage when.....
I take advantage of friends when.....
I feel let down by friends when......
I have been pleasantly surprised by friends who....
If I got married I would want my partner to be......
The sort of friend I believe I am is......

I would be a better friend if I.....
With my friends I usually enjoy.....
I would not help my friends if.....
The most difficult thing about making a new friend is.....
The most difficult thing about starting a friendship with someone of the opposite sex is....
With my friends I feel free to.....
If I disagree with my friends I.......
I find it difficult to disagree with my friends when they......
One thing I believe my friends would say about me is....
I get friends to do what I want by....
In the past a time I felt left out was........
In the past I have left someone out by......
The person I most admire in school is.....
The person I most admire in my community is.....
The sort of person I am inspired by is....
At home the sort of person I am is......
With my friends the sort of person I am is....
With teachers the sort of person I am is.....
The sort of teachers I admire are.....
One thing I would like to change about this school is......
One thing I would like to change about this class is.....
The best thing about where I live is....
The worst thing about where I live is.....
The way I show my family I'm angry is.....
Something I admire about my Mum/Dad/parents is.....
A good time I had with my family was.....
I could laugh with my Mum/Dad about......
I could laugh with my brothers/sisters about....
The thing I admire about my (sibling) is......
The thing that annoys me most about my (sibling) is......
I'm most proud of.....
I'm good/not good at being on my own when......
When I'm on my own I prefer to....
I feel my parents/siblings take advantage of me when.....
I take advantage of my parents/siblings when.....
The family member I would most like to be is......
I wish my parents would......
When I argue with my parents they....
When I argue with my parents I.....
When I argue with my (sibling) I.....
When I argue with my (sibling) my parents.......
Something I rely on my family for is.......
Something I would miss about my (sibling) is.....
Something I would miss about my Mum/Dad is......
I still need adults for..........
One way I am different from other pupils is....
One way I am the same as other pupils is.....
I sometimes wonder how.......
I sometimes wonder why.....
I sometimes wonder if.......

I believe in....
Someone I hope to be like is....
I am worried by....
When I leave this school I hope people will remember me as......
The sort of person I see myself as is....
I am not pleased with myself when......
A time I was brave was......
A fear I would like to overcome is.........
I worry about...
If I were Prime Minister I would......
If I could make changes in this world I would......
What I think about death is.......
Something I intend achieving is.......
Something I have achieved recently is..........
Something I have learned to do recently is.......
Something I think is good about being a boy/girl is.....
Something I would like to do again is...........
Something I will never do again........
Something I avoid doing is........
When kids make mistakes teachers should........
I wish I could.........
If I had three wishes...
A hobby I wish I could do is......
A sport I wish I could do is.....
A place I wish I could visit is....
Someone I wish I could meet is......
Something I wish I could do is......
When I was little I used to wish.......
When I grow up I wish to be...............
Something I wish for my family is...........
Something I wish for my class is............
Something I wish for this school is............
I wish my parents would let me...........
Today I feel....
When I first came to school I felt............
Before I came to this school I felt...........
New experiences/the unknown makes me feel..........
I feel powerless when............
I feel helpless when...........
I feel lonely when.........
I feel concerned for.........
Making decisions makes me feel.........
If I make a mistake I feel...........
My favourite TV programme is........
My favourite book is........
My favourite computer programme is......
My favourite food is........
My favourite time of the year is........
My favourite person in my family is.........
My favourite pop/TV star is........

My favourite time at home is..........
My favourite time at school is.........
My favourite time is.......
My favourite game to play is.......
My favourite things to do with my friends is......
My favourite possession is.....
My favourite toy is.......
My favourite place in my house is......
My favourite place to go is......
My favourite type of weather is........
My favourite thing to wear is........
At home I am good at.....
In school I am good at.....
I like doing....
At home I am not very good at...
At school I am not very good at.....
I dislike doing......
Something I like doing but am not very good at is.......
Something I intend learning is....
I am at my best ....
Something that was a hard decision for me was.....
I would like to take responsibility at home for....
I would like to take responsibility at school for....

Game 1

Take a lucky dip from the pack and use this as the sentence start.

Game 2

Deal the cards so that each participant has a different sentence start.

Game 3

Divide into pairs. Give one card to each pair. The task is to compose two sentences which are common to both - feedback “We are both...” and "We are both..." - one sentence each.

Game 4

Before Circle Time starts give all participants a card and ask them to prepare a picture or a mimed answer to present in the Circle later. The circle members guess the answer.

Activities using the Imagecards

The pictures here are specially chosen to represent a concept without assigning particular characteristics, brand names or identities. For example the image below is always recognised as a car but does not evoke "old red BMW" or "new yellow Fiat".

This neutrality allows participants to attach their own preconceptions. Each will make his or her own valid response. The general aim is to work towards the use of the cards as door openers. At various stages of maturity we can expect different responses. These might follow a development, staged pattern:

"Car."
"We've got a red car."
"We've got a new car and it goes fast."
"My friend's Dad had an accident and he's in hospital."

The "car" is a decreasingly significant part of the response and the experiences and feelings of the speaker become more significant.

Game 1

Give out the cards, one to each participant. Go round in turn starting the sentence with one of the following:
This is my card - it reminds me of..
This is my card - it makes me feel..
This is my card - it makes me want to say..
This is my card - it is important to me because..

Instead of a "pass" allow a "swap".

Game 2

Arrange participants in groups of 5 - 6 and give out a bunch of cards, twice as many as number in the group. Ask the group to sort out the cards so that each person has one which suits him or her. The surplus cards go back into the pack.

Feedback to the whole group with sentence starts as in Game 1.

Game 3

Before the circle starts give out cards, one to each member of the class. Ask them to make pictures of the same object but with more detail... to personalise them. In the circle go round and show both cards.

> *"My card is a spider. I have made it into the spider I saw under my dad's chair last night."*

Game 4

Arrange participants in pairs. Give out one card to each pair and ask them to discuss how similar or different their responses are to the symbol. Feed these back into the whole group.

Activities using the Feeling cards

These cards illustrate a feeling with a cartoon or symbol picture. They are designed to increase the variety and understanding of feelings used. At the opening of the Antidote Conference on The Fourth 'R' - Relationships (Regents College 1998), Elizabeth Hartley-Brewer said,

> *"How can children learn to understand the feelings of others if they do not understand their own feelings first."*

It seemed to make sense until we thought about it and decided it is probably the other way round - most of us have informed our own emotional life by our responses to others. A small child cries, often and for many reasons. She "understands" this feeling. Then she sees an adult cry and her understanding is expanded. The distress or grief assumes an another dimension. This can then be recognised as different from her own crying for tiredness or minor frustration.

Goleman's publication on Emotional Literacy (1995) list the following categories into which feelings can be sorted. The main categories as set out by Daniel Goleman are as follows:

Anger	Sadness	Fear	Enjoyment
Love	Surprise	Disgust	Shame

In Dealing with Feeling, Tina Rae (1998) has produced a complete lesson plan for the twenty feelings appropriate to teach to children.

1. Angry	2. Sad	3. Afraid
4. Happy	5. Surprised	6. Loved
7. Shocked	8. Bored	9. Jealous
10. Ashamed	11. Lonely	12. Greedy
13. Nervous	14. Disappointed	15. Rejected
16. Shy	17. Arrogant	18. Generous
19. Selfish	20. Intimidated.	

The feeling cards provided in this pack have extended the list to 78.

afraid	alone	angry	annoyed
anxious	arrogant	ashamed	attractive
bored	brilliant	busy	calm
cheated	cheerful	clever	confident
confused	contented	cross	determined
different	disappointed	disgusted	excited
exhausted	fascinated	fit	flustered
friendly	frustrated	greedy	generous
happy	healthy	hurt	important
interested	involved	intimidated	irritated
jealous	joyful	lazy	lonely
loved	loving	muddled	nervous
panicked	picked on	popular	proficient
proud	refreshed	rejected	relaxed
restless	sad	selfish	shocked
shy	sick	silly	sleepy
smart	special	surprised	strong
stupid	talkative	tense	thoughtful
threatened	tired	torn	upset
useful	worried		

We suggest that the facilitator carefully checks through the list and makes a selection suitable for the age and maturity of the group.

Game 1

Give out a card to each person in the circle.
Start a sentence completion activity with

The feeling is ______ - I think it means....
The feeling is ______ - it happens when....
The feeling is ______ - when people feel this it makes them....
The feeling is ______ - when I feel like this I usually do ....

Game 2

Before Circle Time put the participants into groups of 2 - 4 and give them a feeling card. Ask them to:

- draw a picture to show the feeling
- write an acrostic poem for the feeling.

This work can be done as individual, pair or group efforts.

Game 3

Deal out a feeling card to each member of the group. Tell them that they will be asked to do a sentence completion - "I feel ___________ when. Instead of a pass offer a swap from the remaining cards.

Game 4

Deal out a set of five cards to each person. Ask the members of the circle to choose two cards each and feed back:

This is how I often feel _______
This is how I rarely feel ________

Game 5

Before the circle ask the young people to work in groups of 4 - 6 with a large sheet of paper. Give out a set of 3 - 4 cards and ask them to make up a story which uses all the cards in a sequence. It can be written, or drawn like a comic strip with speech bubbles. Each group feeds back to the circle.

Game 6

Give out a card to each person in the group. Ask them to decide whether the card is a good feeling, a bad feeling or a neutral feeling.
Use these categories for a mixing up game.

Conclusion

As we write more ideas occur - there are so many ways in which the cards can be used and no doubt the young people will devise their own games and activities. We hope that this resource meets some of the needs you have expressed for additional activities and we would very much like to hear from you about the ways in which you extend Circle Time.

George Robinson and Barbara Maines

Bibliography

Bliss, T. & Tetley, J., (1993) Circle Time
Lucky Duck Publishing.

Bliss, T., Robinson, G. and Maines, B., (1995) Developing Circle Time
Lucky Duck Publishing.

Ballard, J., (1982) Circlebook
Irvington, New York.

Elias, M. J. and Calbby, J., (1992) Building Social Problem Solving Skills: Guidelines from a school based programme, Josey-Bass.

Goleman, D. (1995) Emotional Intelligence Why it can matter more than I.Q.
London, Bloomsbury.

Greenberg, M.T. and Kusche, C.A. (1993) Promoting Social and Emotional Development in Deaf Children. The PATH programme. Seattle. University of California Press.

Mosley, J., (1996) Quality Circle Time.
LDA Cambridge.

Rae, T., (1998) Dealing with Feeling.
Lucky Duck Publishing.

Robinson, G. and Maines, B., (1996) Coming Round to Circle Time video.
Lucky Duck Publishing.

The Sentence Completion cards

A friend is.....

A quality I look for in a friend is......

Something I like to do with friends is......

Something I like to do with my best friend is......

The sort of people I like best are....

The sort of person I would trust is....

I respect friends who.....

If a friend has deceived me.....

The way I show my friends I'm angry is......

I laugh with my friends about......

Something my friends do that makes me laugh is.....

The kind of behaviour I would expect from my friends towards me is......

The kind of behaviour I prefer to see from my friends when we are out is.....

If my friends fall out I try to get them back together by....

An irritating habit that would turn me off could be....

Friends take advantage when.....

I take advantage of friends when.....

I feel let down by friends when......

I have been pleasantly surprised by friends who....

If I got married I would want my partner to be......

The sort of friend I believe I am is......

I would be a better friend if I.....

With my friends I usually enjoy.....

I would not help my friends if.....

The most difficult thing about making a new friend is.....

The most difficult thing about starting a friendship with someone of the opposite sex is....

With my friends I feel free to.....

If I disagree with my friends I.......

I find it difficult to disagree with my friends when they......

One thing I believe my friends would say about me is....

I get friends to do what I want by....

In the past I felt left out when........

In the past I have left someone out by......

The person I most admire in school is.....

The person I most admire in my community is.....

The sort of person I am inspired by is....

At home the sort of person I am is......

With my friends the sort of person I am is....

With teachers the sort of person I am is.....

The sort of teachers I admire are.....

One thing I would like to change about this school is......

One thing I would like to change about this class is.....

The best thing about where I live is....

The worst thing about where I live is.....

The way I show my family I'm angry is.....

Something I admire about my Mum/Dad/parents is.....

A good time I had with my family was.....

I could laugh with my Mum/Dad about......

I could laugh with my brothers/sisters about....

The thing I admire about my (sibling) is......

The thing that annoys me most about my (sibling) is......

I'm most proud of.....

I'm good/not good at being on my own when......

When I'm on my own I prefer to....

I feel my parents/siblings take advantage of me when.....

I take advantage of my parents/siblings when.....

The family member I would most like to be is......

I wish my parents would......

When I argue with my parents they....

When I argue with my parents I.....

When I argue with my (sibling) I.....

When I argue with my (sibling) my parents.......

Something I rely on my family for is.......

Something I would miss about my (sibling) is.....

Something I would miss about my Mum/Dad is......

I still need adults for..........

One way I am different from other pupils is....

One way I am the same as other pupils is.....

I sometimes wonder how.......

I sometimes wonder why.....

I sometimes wonder if.......

I believe in....

Someone I hope to be like is....

I am worried by....

When I leave this school I hope people will remember me as......

The sort of person I see myself as is....

I am not pleased with myself when......

A time I was brave was......

A fear I would like to overcome is.........

I worry about...

If I were Prime Minister I would......

If I could make changes in this world I would......

What I think about death is.......

Something I intend achieving is.......

Something I have achieved recently is.........

Something I have learned to do recently is.......

Something I think is good about being a boy/girl is.....

Something I would like to do again is..........

Something I will never do again........

Something I avoid doing is........

When kids make mistakes teachers should........

I wish I could.........

If I had three wishes...

A hobby I wish I could do is......

A sport I wish I could do is......

A place I wish I could visit is....

Someone I wish I could meet is......

Something I wish I could do is......

When I was little I used to wish.......

When I grow up I wish to be...............

Something I wish for my family is..........

Something I wish for my class is............

Something I wish for this school is............

I wish my parents would let me...........

Today I feel....

When I first came to school I felt...........

Before I came to this school I felt...........

New experiences/the unknown makes me feel..........

I feel powerless when...........

I feel helpless when...........

I feel lonely when.........

I feel concerned for.........

Making decisions makes me feel.........

If I make a mistake I feel..........

My favourite TV programme is........

My favourite book is........

My favourite computer programme is......

My favourite food is........

My favourite time of the year is........

My favourite person in my family is.........

My favourite pop/TV star is........

My favourite time at home is.........

My favourite time at school is.........

My favourite time is.......

My favourite game to play is.......

My favourite things to do with my friends is......

My favourite possession is.....

My favourite toy is.......

My favourite place in my house is......

My favourite place to go is......

My favourite type of weather is........

My favourite thing to wear is........

At home I am good at.......

In school I am good at.....

I like doing....

At home I am not very good at...

At school I am not very good at.....

I dislike doing......

Something I like doing but am not very good at is.......

Something I intend learning is....

I am at my best ....

Something that was a hard decision for me was.....

I would like to take responsibility at home for....

I would like to take responsibility at school for....

The Image cards

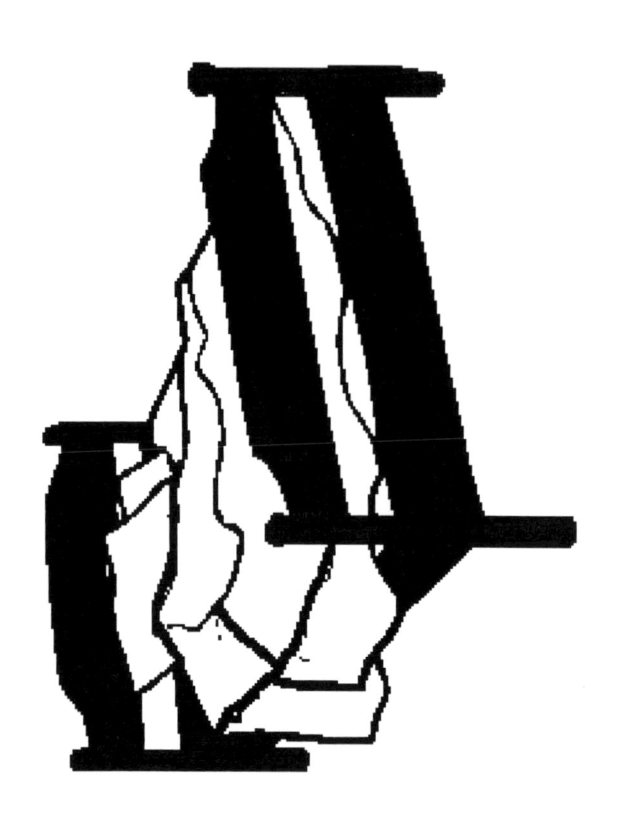

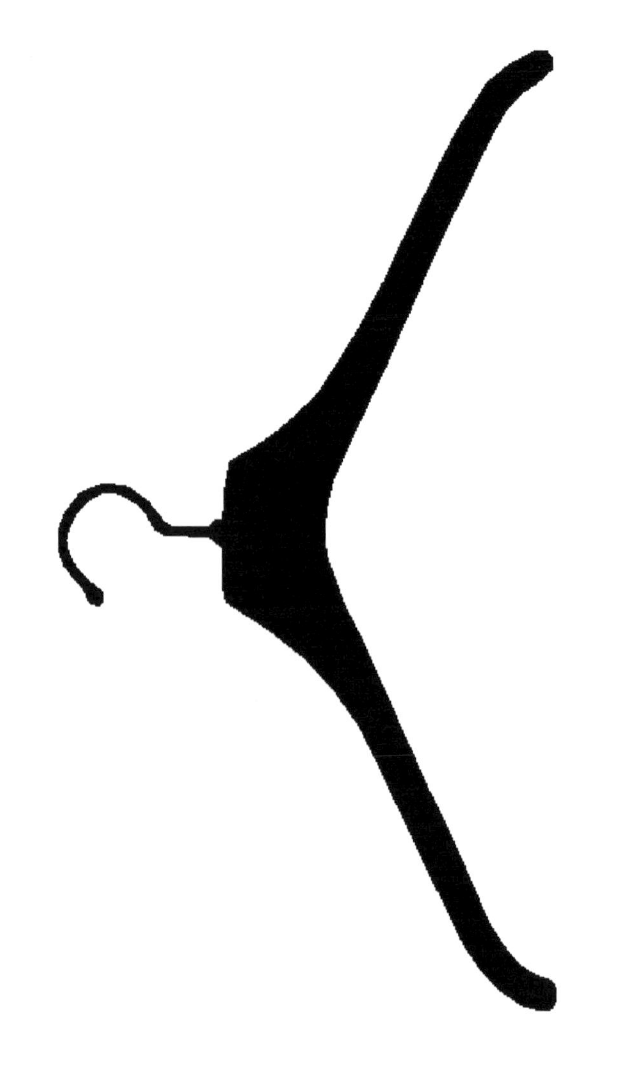

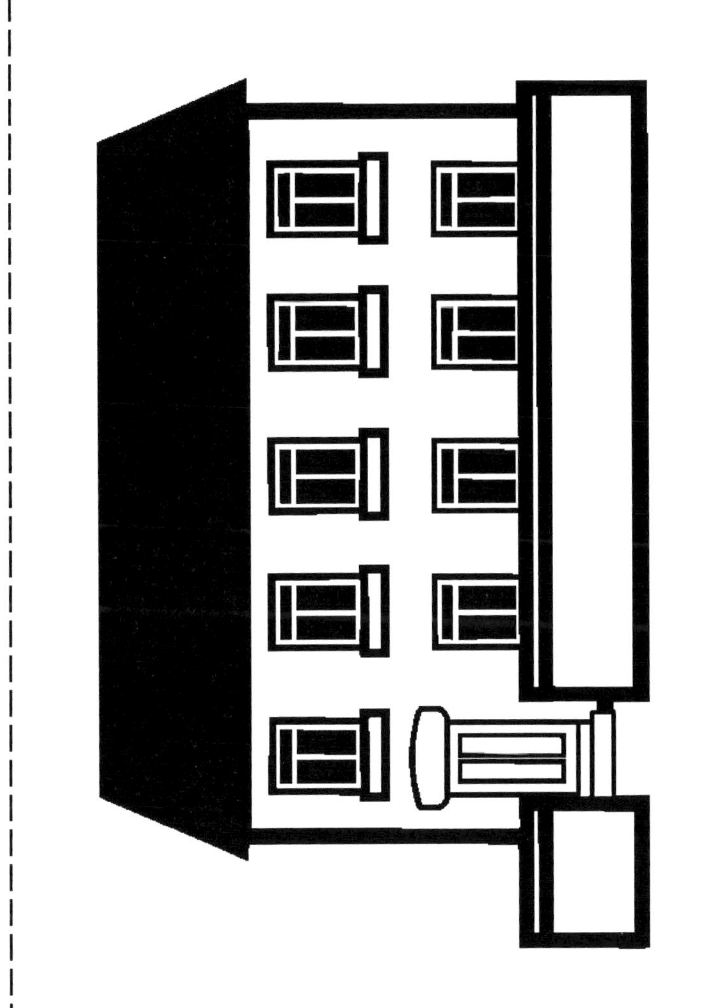

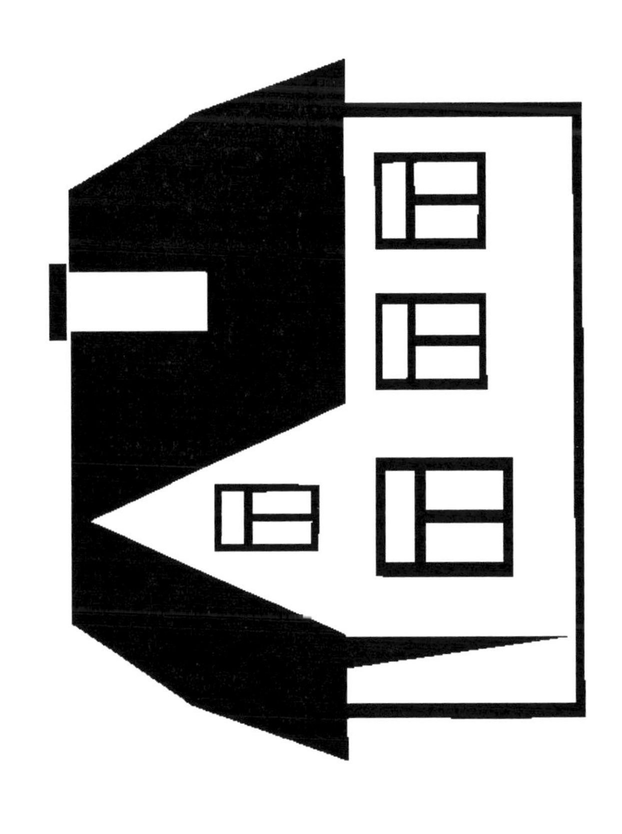

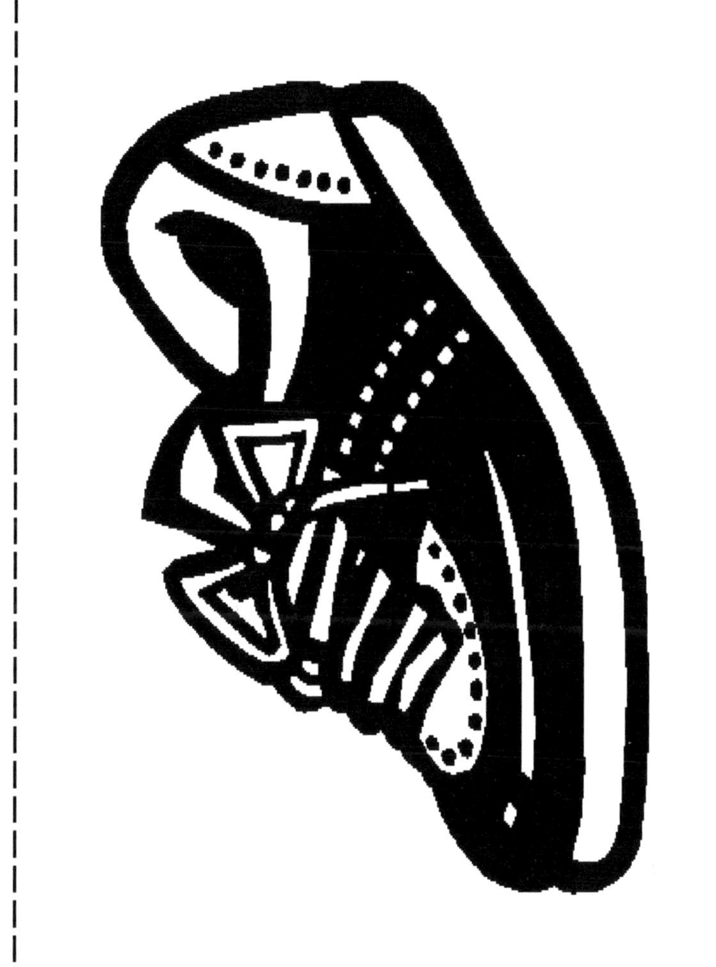

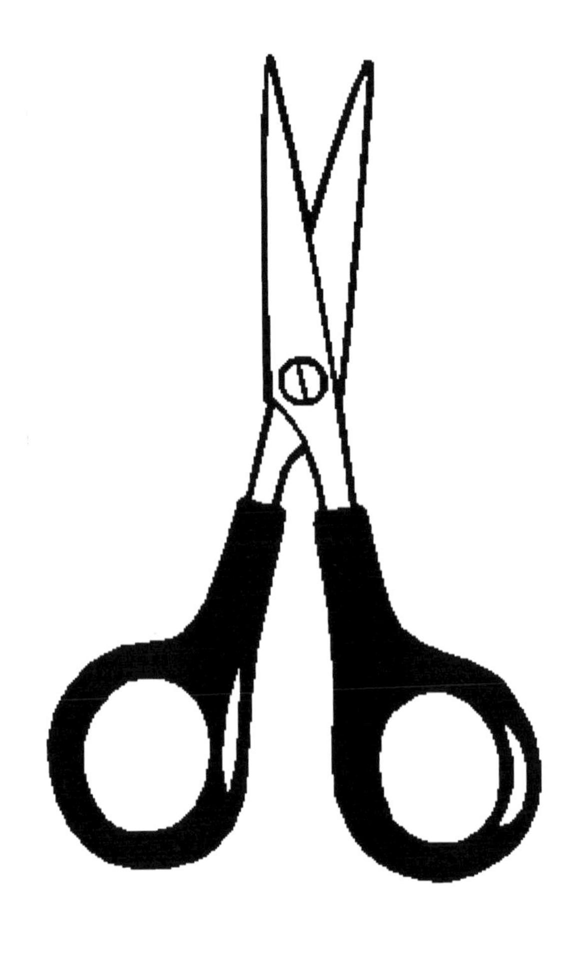
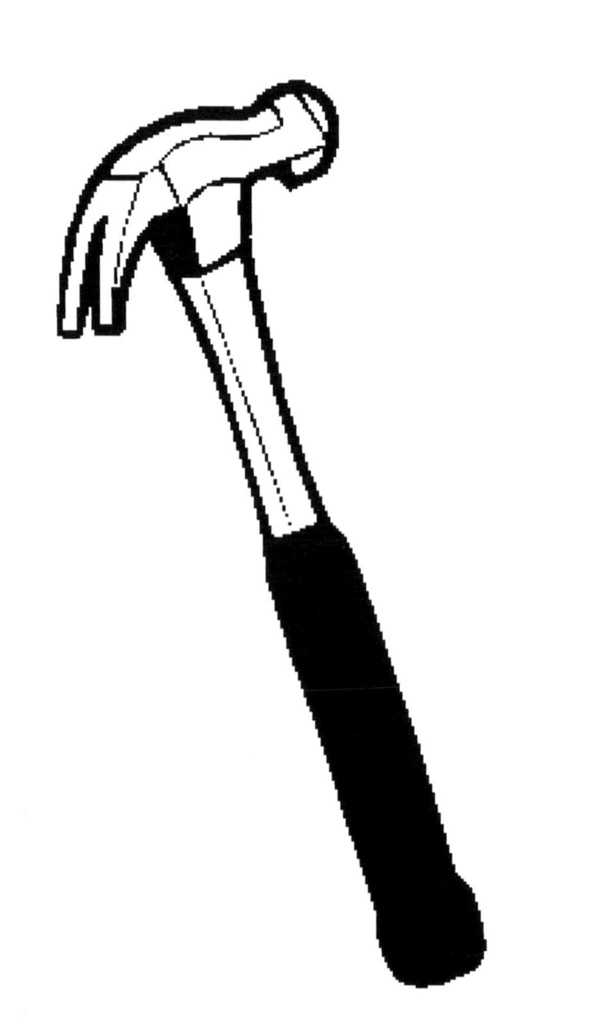

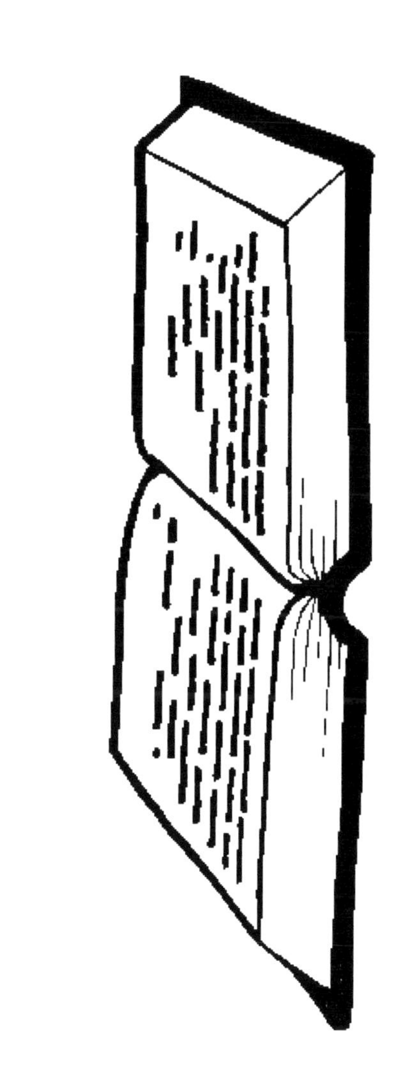

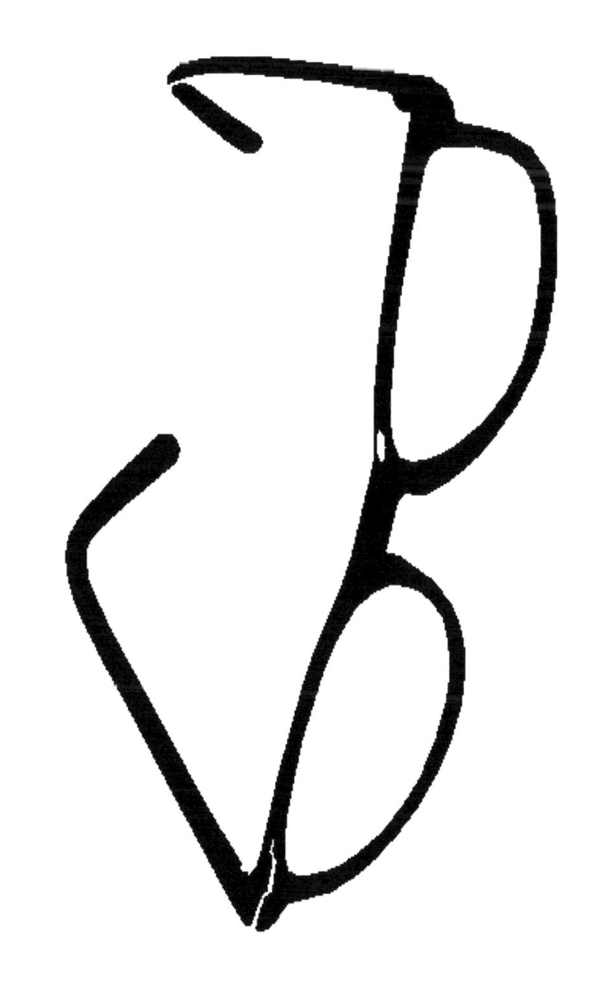

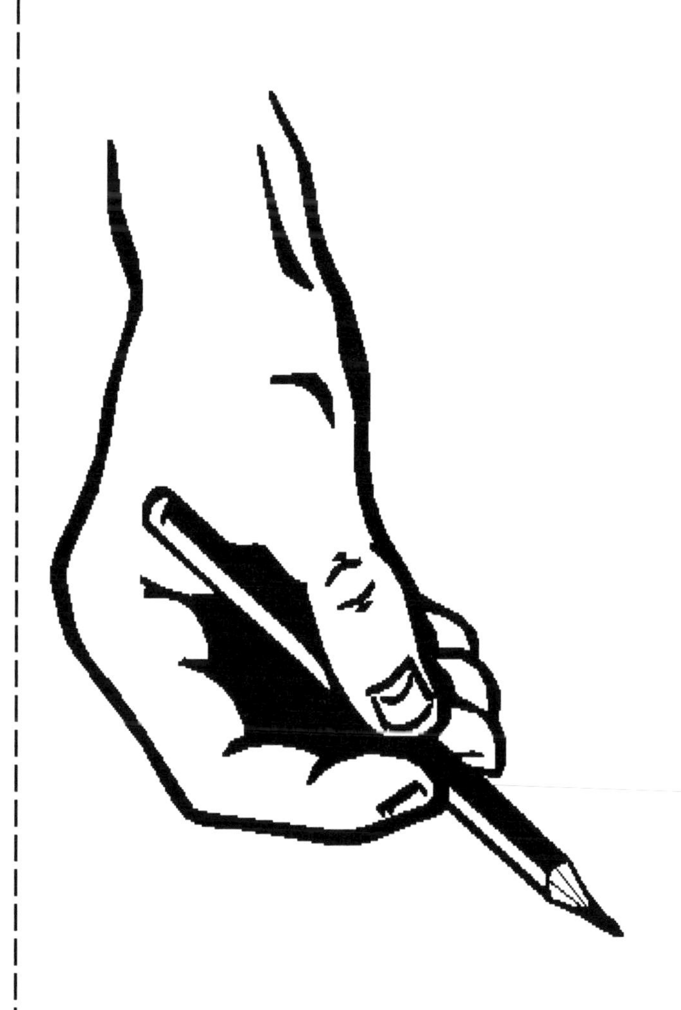

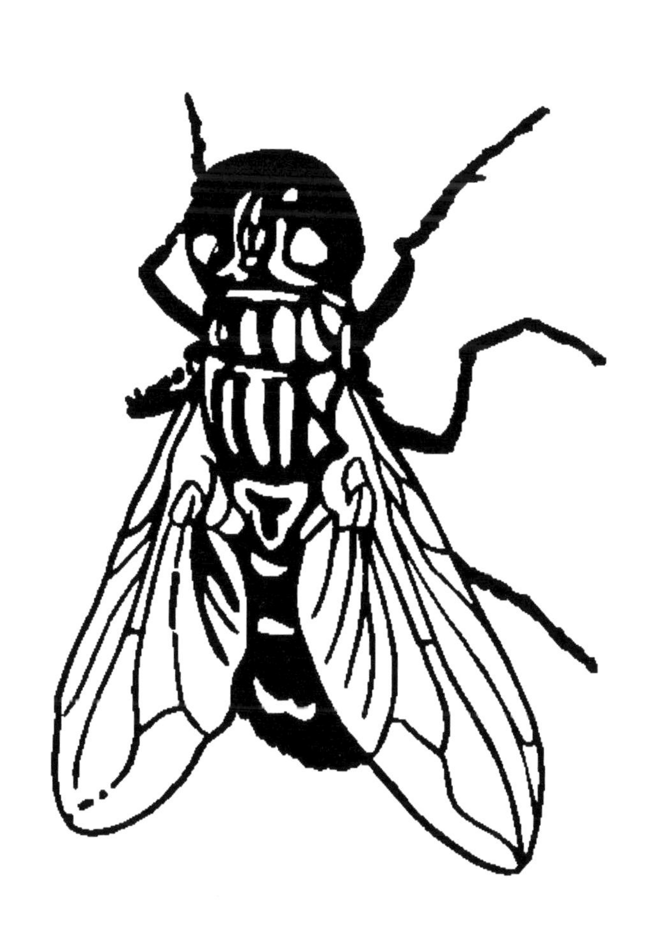

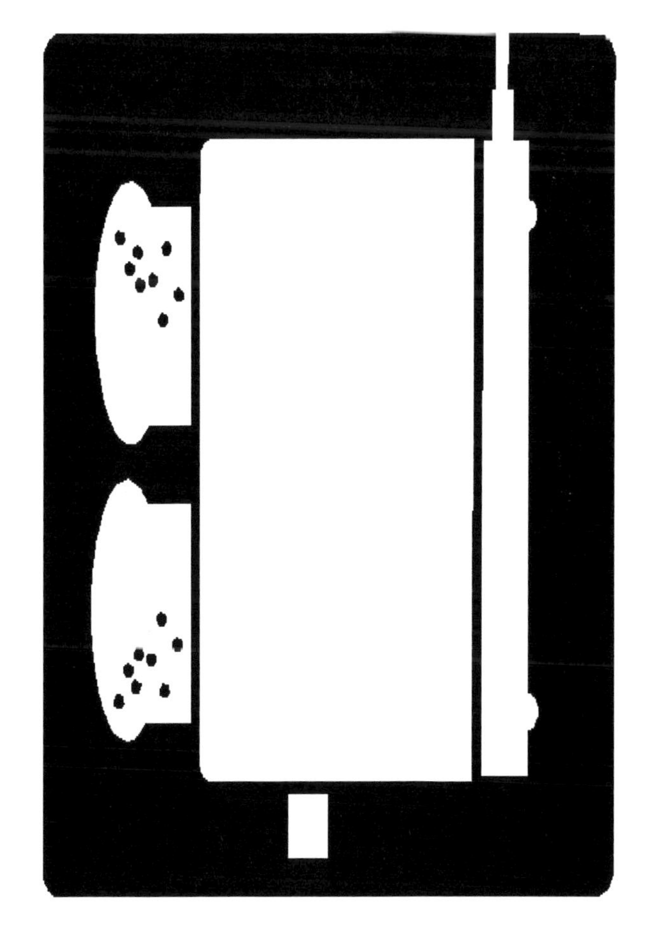

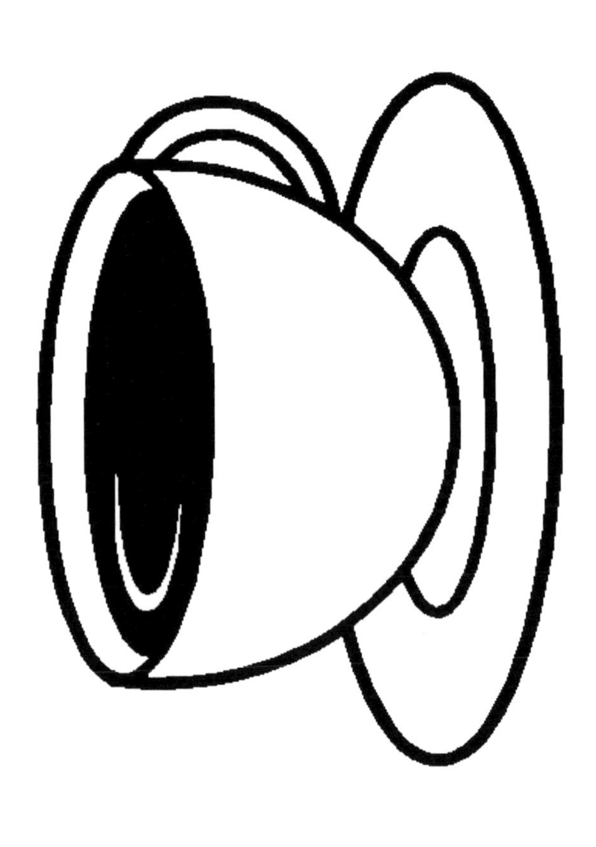

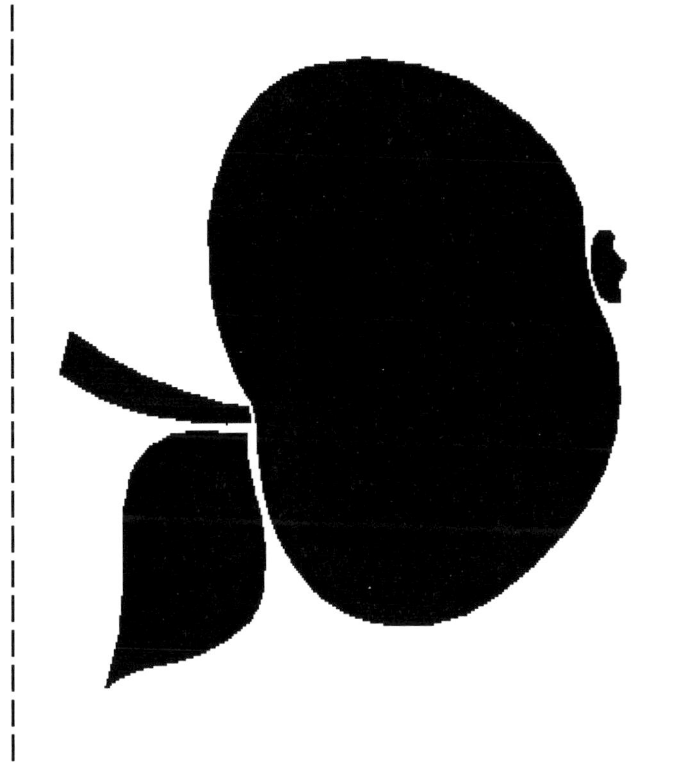
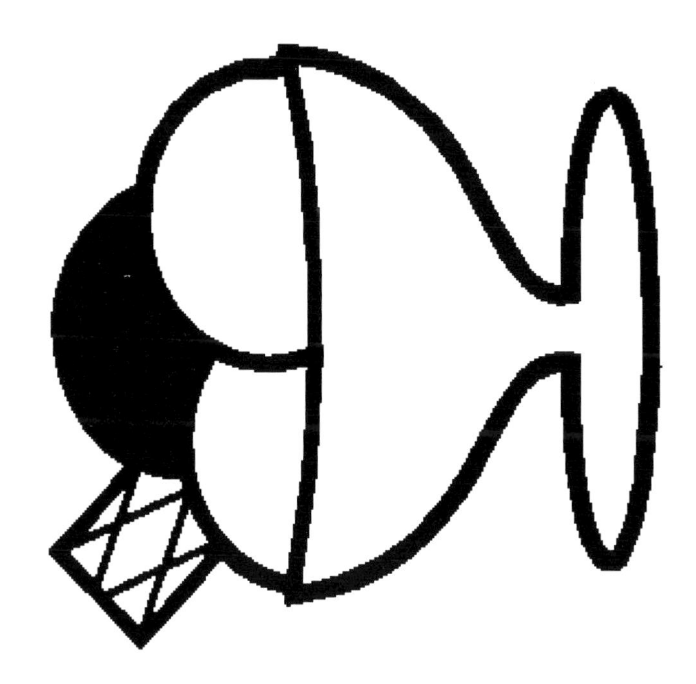

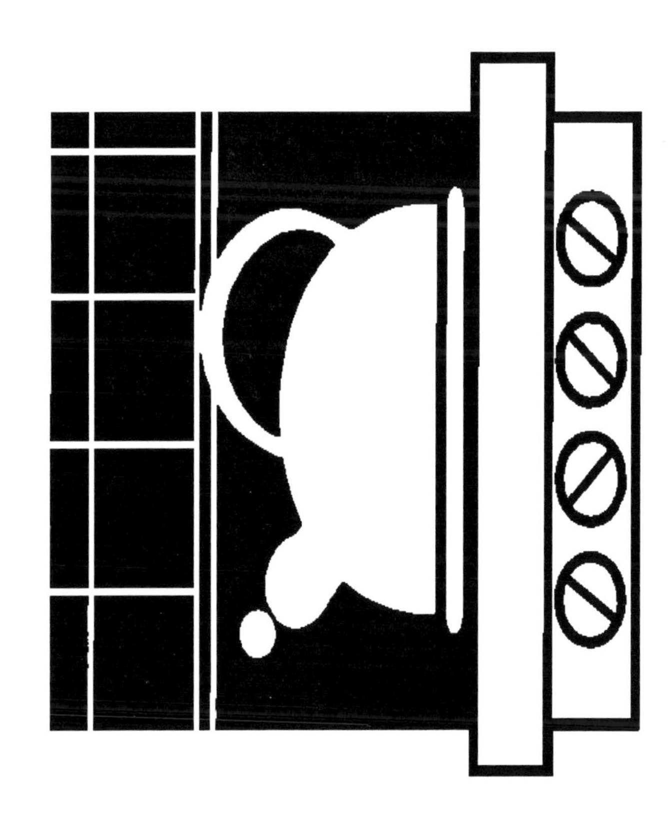

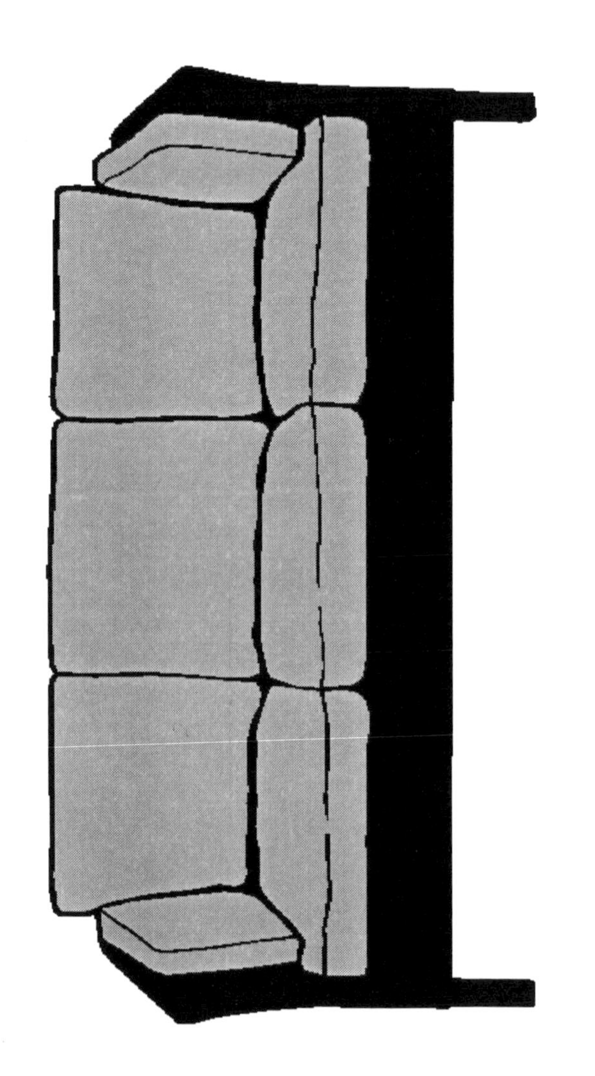

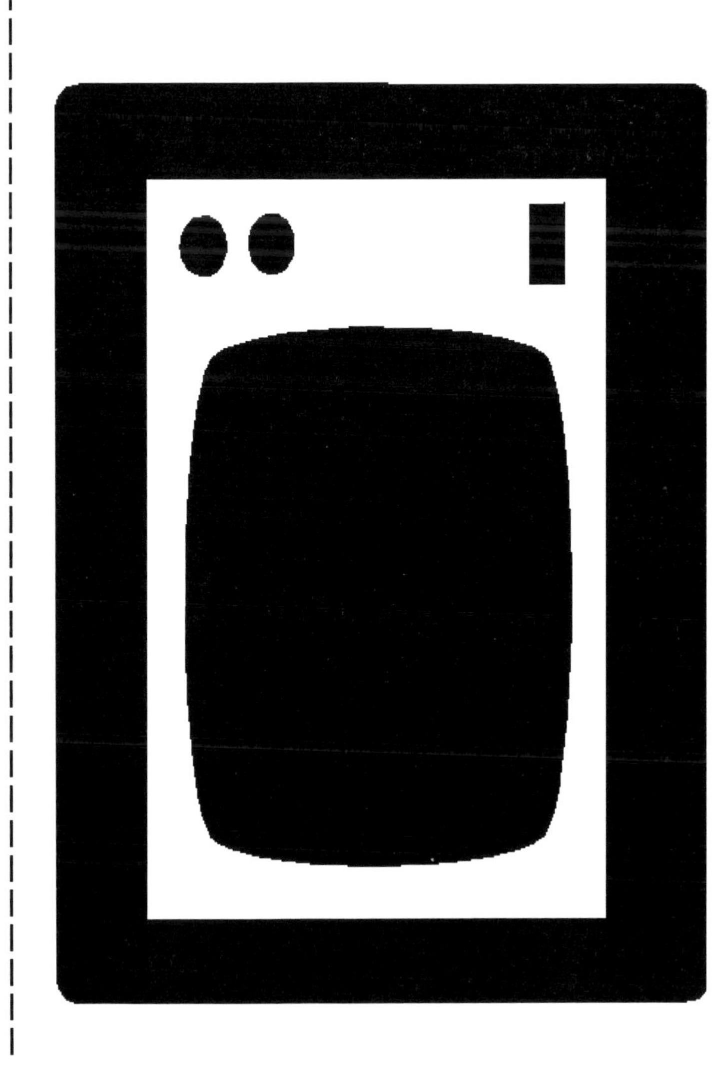

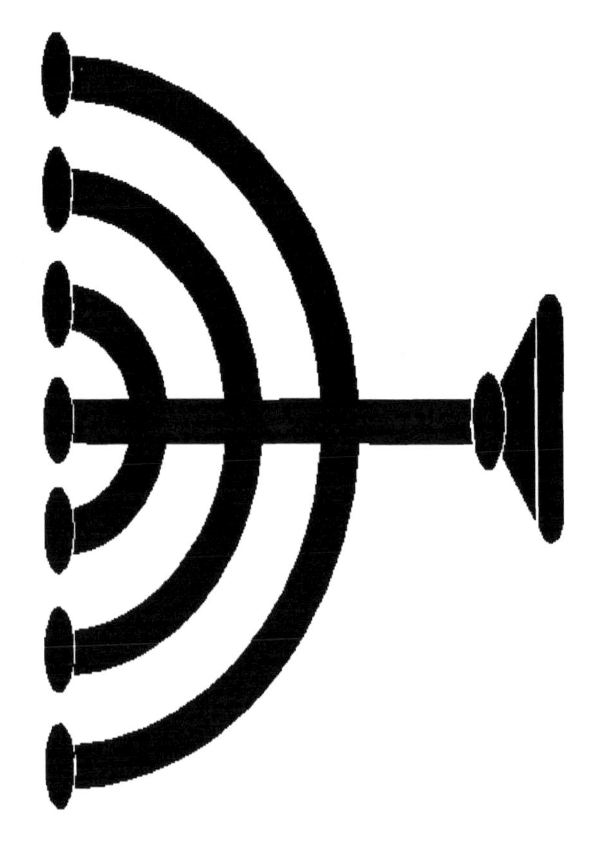

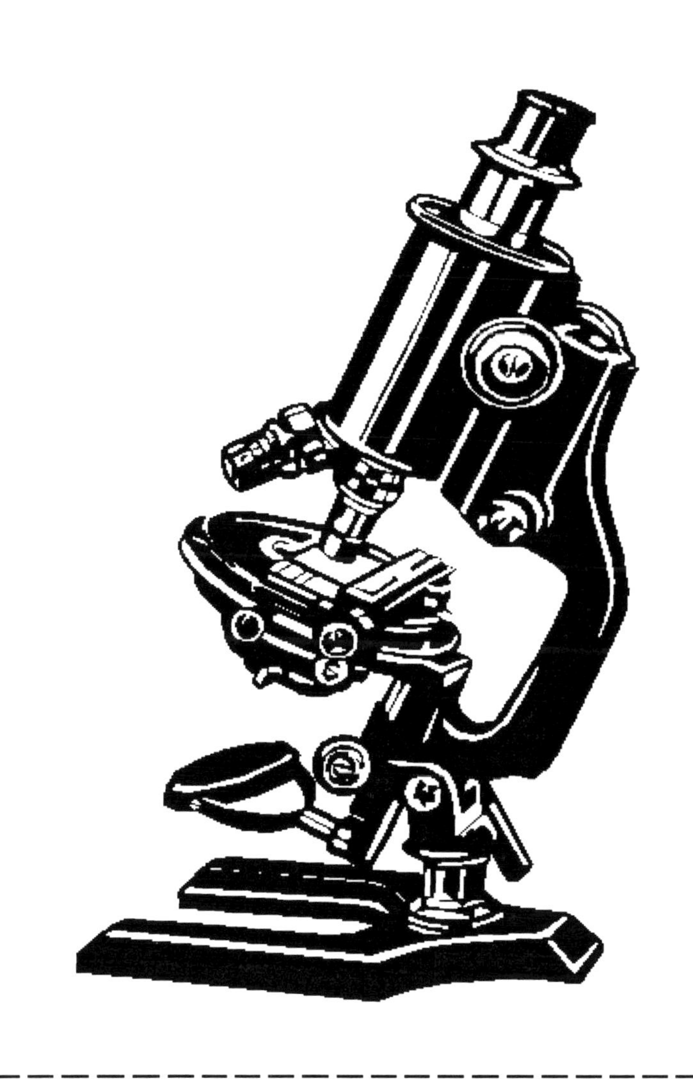

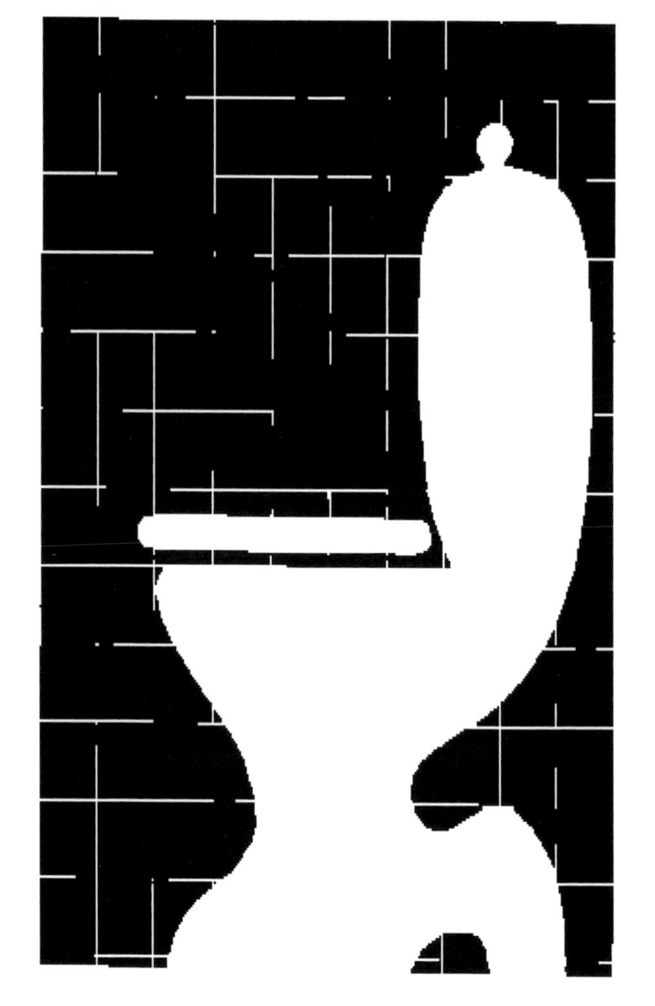

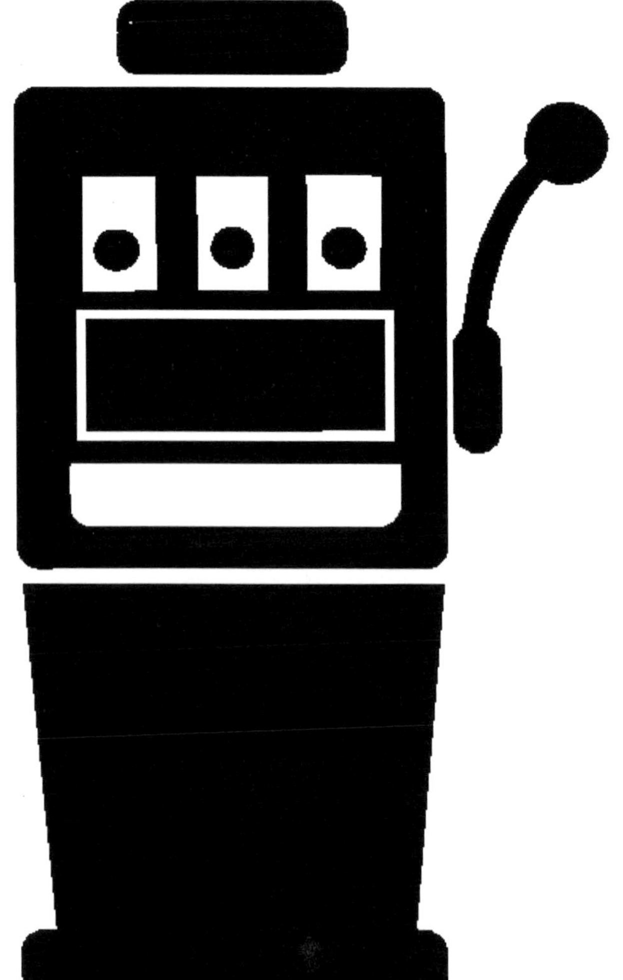

The Feeling cards

Friendly

Sad

Silly

Loving

Worried

Smart

Healthy

Hurt

Angry

Lazy

Sick

Sleepy

Attractive

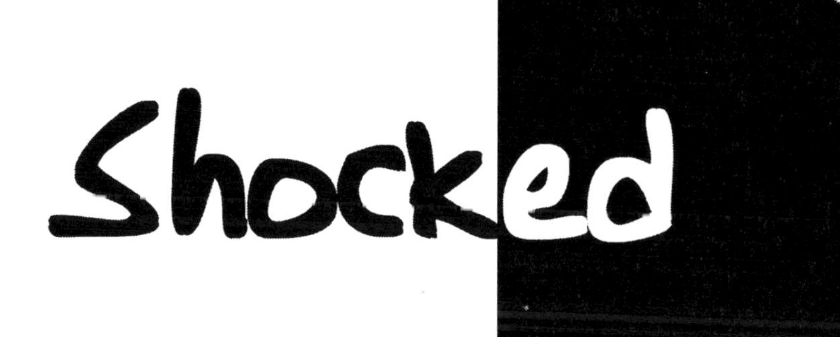

Shocked

Proud

Bored

Alone

Calm

Determined

Disgusted

Excited

Fascinated

Joyful

Lonely

Proficient

Restless

Strong

Thoughtful

Interested

Suprised

Happy

Cross

Cheerful

Tired

Panicked

Relaxed

Ashamed

Threatened

Refreshed

Popular

Clever

Stupid

Picked on

Muddled

Involved

Upset

Nervous

Exhausted

Irritated

Contented

Afraid

Annoyed

Frustrated

Confident

Useful

Tense

Shy

Special

Talkative

Fit

Flustered

Cheated

Anxious

Busy

Greedy

Disappointed

Arrogant

Different

Loved

Intimidated

Rejected

Jealous

Torn

Selfish

Brilliant

Important

Generous